Your Noisy Eyes

Heath Brougher

Stay Weird and Keep Writing
Print Co

Oklahoma

USA

To all the
fool wishes,

Stay Weird and Keep Writing Print Co
Non-Profit Entity

stayweirdandkeepwriting@mail.com

stayweirdandkeepwriting.wordpress.com

4208 NW 56th
Oklahoma City, OK 73112
USA
(405) 889-9583

Edited By Patrick Jordan

Cover art by Bree
Her work can be found at theartistbree.com
greenpandapress@gmail.com

First Printing Edition

Other works by the same author:

"A Curmudgeon is Born" can be found at *Yellow Chair Review's* website at:

- http://www.yellowchairreview.com/availabl e-titles-chapbooks &

- Amazon.com: https://www.amazon.com/Curmudgeon-born-Heath-Brougher/dp/0692718605/ref=sr_1_1?ie=UT F8&qid=1483926538&sr=8-1&keywords=Heath+Brougher

Heath Brougher can also be found on Facebook:

https://www.facebook.com/heath.brougher

3

ACKNOWLEDGEMENTS

"2" was originally published in *The Bitchin Kitsch*.

"8" was originally published in *Mobius: A Journal of Social Change*.

"9" and "10" were originally published in *Dead Snakes Literary Journal.*

Ten of these poems originally appeared in the chapbook *"Digging for Fire"* (Stay Weird and Keep Writing Print Co)

1

Scanning across the loam and junkyards soon enough to be nonexistent. That bomb planted deep within the Earth awaits. People look back because that is all they can do. People. Us. We reminisce. We reminisce what our eyes have recorded throughout our lives. The camera lens looks like a black eye. The camera lens looks like a mouth wide open. The camera lens looks like O. The camera lens looks like an eyeball. The eyes record the images that make up a life. The eyes record the images that cross its path. The eyes record the perceptions. The eyes record the perception that frames the life. The eyes record the Life Itself and backlogs the images for future use. For future reminiscence.

2

Even the bombs with the longest wicks will still one day explode. The seeds of these bombs have already been planted. The seeds of these bombs have already been laid out in the soil. The seeds of these bombs are just waiting and waiting. The seeds of these bombs are just moving through time.

3

The misshapen camera snaps the ugly photo.
The end is not yet ended. The bones of an
oriole are found among the ruins. The cow
tastes the sting of summer and cocktails of
chemicals in the creek water. The clatter of the
squawk-box is ignited. We reminisce us. We
read the blotches of a soup galaxy. The pawn
dangles the dog by its leash in mid-air. With
no one listening the mega-phone eventually
eats itself. The mega-phone screams so loudly
it makes its own ears bleed. Not a single head
is turned. This pales in comparison to the
Great Noise that is on its way.

4

The glass jar never ending. The glass jaw never ending. This sphere is the only sphere we know of. The wine attempts. Somehow pours itself. We are not pictures and we are not in them. The paintbrush is obsolete. We picture ourselves much more accurately and dishonest than ever before. The darkroom is null and void.

5

With the higher altitude we understand less oxygen. But it is the meat which really understands less oxygen. A clover. A hoof. Neither of mine or yours. Broken but broken gently. Smashed but smashed silently and absurdly wondering about the frame and how to frame this situation.

6

The profligate warmers opened the door for the droves of doves. A tooth-o-scope repealed the enamel as the incision was inserted in the dirt of the gum's ground. The quiet bomb sat at full attention ticking its life away. The all it's life would ever be. The envelopment of life that it would attain when the ticking ran out.

7

The camera inside the eye of the fish takes pictures its entire life. The quaalude-eating seagulls don't explode. Instead they cry tears of sobriety into the ocean. [The coin. The O-Coin] The ocean doesn't care. The dropped-into-the-water cracker becomes so saltine that it bloats and softens and dissolves itself. The whales continue to talk in their cello-voices. Sometimes they surface to take pictures with their eyes. If they die before detonation all their pictures end up on the ocean floor slowly rotting away to nothingness. If they die before the detonation their pictures will have been recorded.

8

The necessity of the imminent visualization of the bomb by the brain. The importance of the visualization of the bomb by the brain. The necessity of planning ahead so as to not be so taken aback when the bomb detonates. The probing thought can get distracted by the other things made of roses and retrospection of fond memories and troughs of entrails seen through the dust of time. Yes we reminisce us. The probing thought can be diverted and sent down steel pipelines that endlessly flow meat throughout their circular hallways. There is such necessity of the importance of the imminent visualization of the bomb. Necessity. Preoccupation. Even obsession with the bomb and how to find it and make its explosion quit the Earth. Only then will the nothingness be safe.

9

In a dream the bomb went off underwater.
The trees of the ocean shook as if in the
hardest of gales. The trees of the ocean shook
and were uprooted as if an atomic blast had
suddenly gone off. The trees of the ocean were
torn from their roots and swirled in the slow-
motion chaos of the sky of the ocean. The
octopuses' eggs were swept from their gardens.
There was disaster and calamity and shock in
the voice of the whales. The yelling cellos of
the sea.

10

The out-pulsing thought hit the lonesome highway of the Intellect. The umber and ochre dogs faded to pieces of fiddlesticks. The thought was beyond the Great Siberian Novel. The thought drove right through the magnanimity of diamond doors. The thought wore no blood and was a perfect parabola. The thought flew out into the comprehension of God.

11

The motive drove with perfect vision into the bile house. The motive drove with perfect vision into the brick and glass and Consciousness. The one realized that this is what one must do to peel open the mirror of Truth no matter how grotesque it may be and take it in. Take its picture with your mind. This means that the Earth is barely documented. This means that the motive may live there with Epiphany itself.

12

The air kept spinning. The soul is resting easier in the napalm of your hand. The mercurial rain feeds the steel trees as the rubber camera-mouthed walruses go back to splashing in the Chinese milk just a semen-sore of their half-cousins. The cows drink of the fracture on the basis daily. The red crosses and crescents turn ruddier by the day and await the night's cacophonic symphony of bombs.

The Dizzitorium ate the pandemonium right from the child's hand only to vomit it back up in chunk-form of man fighting man. Religion fighting other religion. The this-is-how-it-goes-and-always-went continued. These battles always seeming to be the recipients of a form of nostalgic and heroic reminiscence. Killing is looked upon as heroic. This is part of the grotesque Truth which must be taken in when they eyes force themselves to record the Truths. Deceit relies on the ability of Truth to hurt you as a way to keep you from examining it. You must learn to take in the Truth no matter how painful it may be. It is the only way to move forward.

14

The home-made space slapped the forwarding thought with anvils. The trees recorded the wind. The spinach spun in tornadoes of humming green. The forwarding thought teetered for a second. The forwarding thought re-grounded itself in the Truth as the estuaries of brain-rot summoned the rats to their daily allowance of nibbling. Many snapshots were taken.

15

The Universal blast will knock out all electricity and Consciousness.

16

The spinning took to its feet and ate flimsy sky-falls. The robust percussion rolled its tongue as it counted the brains. The robust percussion was still not satisfied. The picture of the picture continued to develop itself. The ransom of the night-tiller plummeted upon the emergence of dawn. The rewarming began taking its toll on the Earth.

17

The picture of the eye hung from the wall at a crooked angle. The picture of the eye hung on the wall was still able to follow you wherever you went in the room.

The pivotal pushed-forward thought
continues to stretch like bent snow-laden
limbs and the Universe. The fish swim. The
fish soar in the slow sky of the ocean. The cone
suddenly becomes encased in coldness. The
convex lens of the fish's eye is snapping away
like an insta-recorder. It is recording life itself
and maybe more. It is recording life itself and
maybe the answer of just how to detonate the
bomb.

19

The spiral of the mind is in full bloom. The berries are redder than the deepest of all that is rubicund. The brain charges the electricity of the eyes. All the simultaneous motion and inertia is noted and documented.

20

The probing thought keeps moving through
the bomb and the womb. The probing thought
finds mob bombs and bird's eyes. The probing
thought keeps moving through the mobs and
the ear drums and bird eyes. The probing
thought keeps moving through time capsules
and destructive rasp. The probing thought
keeps moving through the possibility of
Universal repetition.

The vexing matter is sustained. The matter
that vexes the mind is sustained. The
confusion that tries to control can occasionally
mutate and give birth to Epiphanies. The
confounding vexation that tries to keep the
camera lens shut sometimes conjures
epiphanic beings to pry the lens open again.
The time to detonation continues to tick away.
The time to detonation breezes by our every
breath. We are mostly oblivious but we know
it is there in that twitching of our eyes [always
a reminder]. There were bird's eyes and long
skeins of zeros flowing outward like an ocean.
We need to constantly tell ourselves to sieve
through the light and look for it. We need to
constantly reminisce ourselves to see it. To
spell it out with our eyes. To spill it out of our
eyes so it can be seen and comprehended.

22

The owl's oval eyes capture the world of natural espionage in such a high resolution. The owl's oval eyes are able to see in the dark a garden of lightlessness as if wearing night-vision goggles. Even better actually. The owl's oval eyes can see the microbes and germs on the face of a human being. Nothing can be anything without memory and sensation. These are our perceptions. These are all we have.

The time continuing the ongoing unheard
ticking. The ongoing time has no ears or eyes
in the metaphysical sense but in the natural
and human sense it does. The wick can be
found and traced. The wick can become the
most serious game of hide-and-go-seek
Mankind has ever played.

24

If the explosion had occurred underwater it would have been as if the ocean was vomiting up a large portion of itself. If it did it would have been like water spitting out water. It would have been something similar to the Gulf of Mexico during the last days of the dinosaurs. All the pictures taken of those days are now fossilized. All those direct portraits and notes lost and gone forever.

25

There may be occasional worms that dig their
ant-like farms right around the bomb. There
may be moles that dig right around it but
never see it because they are sightless. Blind as
a mole. But if and/or when it detonates even
creatures as deaf as a germ will hear its
explosion. Reminiscence of the streetlight
illumed in all its luster and luminosity. Bright
death brought straight to your eyes unframed.
Live, noted, and then
.....[static].....[nothingness].....

26

We could suck in the eye's glaring of the oval
bubbles of Ovid but even the most peaceful
bubble eventually bursts. The eyes sucking in
of Ovid's oval path that he must have worn
while pacing alone in deep thought. In deep
thought and capturing the images of those
deep thoughts with his mind.

27

The exactitude of the convex hawk's eye
protruded in a microscopic way out into the
spherical Earth. The dirt lay still soon ready to
bloom brown and dead when the seed of the
bomb's wick sizzled its way to detonation. The
punch-card ballots in the hands of Floridians
were dimpled and pregnant with vote. The
mainstream knew there was a detonation
coming but decided to look away. It muzzled
itself. It muffled itself. It deadened itself to
such a degree that it was enveloped by the
oblivion of false reality. The false realities that
flickered on a screen of moving images. Not
just one silent and unmoving picture but a
picture made of sound and motion. A slice of a
schism. The difference between the eagle and
the mole was palpable.

28

The cacophony yet to come will be the ultimate apex. The cacophony yet to come will ring so loudly it will blind eyes and deafen germs. The cacophony yet to come will be so bright and hot it will melt the flesh right off the skin. The cacophony yet to come will turn everything into something beyond even the nothingness of dust. The cacophony yet to come will dissolve even the strongest photogene. The cacophony yet to come will erase the All of Everything.

29

[[But what? What if we're wrong? What if the
wick of the bomb is made of veins? What if the
wick of the bomb is made of the stringy
insides of the human body? What if the wick
of the bomb is metaphysical and no picture
can be taken? What if the wick of the bomb
turns out to be made of some kind of
Pantheistic destiny itself? What if the wick of
the bomb has already been smothered?]]

30

The skeins and spheres are in the ripples of the soup. The skeins and spheres are still structurally sound. The soupy skeins and spheres still resemble planets and solar systems when beads of sweat drip into the bowl. The oval bowl. Soon to be disrupted. Soon to be a loud blare and brightness before the eyes. What happens then? What happens when even the photogenes are forever wiped clear and blank?

31

Do the laws of physics exist in the black hole of your giant pupils? What happens when we are left not even with photogenes? Without any recall whatsoever? When we come face to face with nonexistence? No more perception and communication and images and thoughts and a big eraser that won't exist because nothing will be there to be perceived and documented.

32

The hand reaches deep into the wall where the eyes can't see. The hand feels nothing. With the hand feeling nothing the eye of the mind is led to believe that nothing is there. The perception of nothingness is born from what the hand can't feel and the eyes can't see and the mind can't perceive. The perception of nothingness is a trick the human mind can play on itself.

33

So it is possible that the words and ideas
themselves are the bombs and we've been
exploding our entire lives. The whole theory
of a long-burning wick could just be a dense
ruse to shroud the Truth from ever finding
Consciousness. This realization forms in the
image of a light-bulb shattering above our
heads and spilling jagged seeds of glass onto
our brains. The possibility of an entire life
spent walking in the wrong direction.

Made in the USA
Middletown, DE
10 March 2017